WORKBOOK

LEVEL A

A Pig Can Jig

by Donald Rasmussen and Lynn Goldberg

Columbus, Ohio

A Division of The McGraw·Hill Companies

Printed in the United States of America.

Send all inquiries to:
SRA/McGraw-Hill
250 Old Wilson Bridge Road, Suite 310
Worthington, OH 43085

ISBN 0-02-6840057

1 2 3 4 5 6 7 8 9 0   DBH   05 04 03 02 01 00 99

ran

can

Dan

fan

man

PURPOSES OF THIS PAGE
1. to promote automatic word recognition
2. to promote word comprehension through picture associations

SECTION 1 LETTER-SOUND CONTENT
New: CVC spelling pattern -an (/an)
Medial vowel letter a as in pan
Initial consonant letters c, d, f, m, r
Final consonant letter n

1

(can)

Dan

ran

fan

ran

man

fan

Dan

ran

can

man

ran

PURPOSES OF THIS PAGE
1. to promote automatic word recognition
2. to contrast words that differ only in their initial consonants
3. to promote word comprehension through picture associations

SECTION 1 LETTER-SOUND CONTENT
New: CVC spelling pattern -an (fan)
Medial vowel letter a as in pan
Initial consonant letters c, d, f, m, r
Final consonant letter n

 Dan ran.

 I can fan.

 The man ran.

 Dan can fan.

 I can fan.

 Dan ran.

 The man ran.

 Dan can fan.

PURPOSES OF THIS PAGE
1. to promote automatic word recognition within sentences
2. to promote sentence comprehension through picture associations

SECTION 1 LETTER-SOUND CONTENT
New: CVC spelling pattern -an (fan)
Medial vowel letter *a* as in *pan*
Initial consonant letters c, d, f, m, r
Final consonant letter n

3

1

○ Dan can fan the man.

○ I ran.

○ Dan ran.

○ The man can fan.

○ I can fan.

○ The man ran.

○ The man can fan Dan.

○ Dan ran.

PURPOSES OF THIS PAGE
1. to promote automatic word recognition within sentences
2. to promote sentence comprehension through picture associations

SECTION 1 LETTER-SOUND CONTENT
New: CVC spelling pattern -an (fan)
Medial vowel letter *a* as in *pan*
Initial consonant letters *c, d, l, m, r*
Final consonant letter *n*

SECTION 1 LETTER-SOUND CONTENT
New: CVC spelling pattern -*an (fan)*
Medial vowel letter *a* as in *pan*
Initial consonant letters *c, d, f, m, r*
Final consonant letter *n*

PURPOSES OF THIS PAGE
1. to promote automatic word recognition within sentences
2. to promote sentence comprehension through picture associations
3. to give practice in picture interpretation

1

2

3

4

4 The man ran.

☐ I can fan.

☐ The man can fan Dan.

☐ Dan ran.

2

Nan

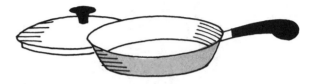

pan

Dan

van

can

PURPOSES OF THIS PAGE
1. to promote automatic word recognition
2. to promote word comprehension through picture associations

SECTION 2 LETTER-SOUND CONTENT
Review: CVC spelling pattern -an (fan)
New: Previously introduced consonant letters
New: Initial consonant letters n, p, v

 van

fan

 can

ran

 pan

ran

 Nan

Dan

 tan

man

 van

pan

2

⊗ **the van**

○ **the fan**

○ **the man**

○ **the fan**

○ **the pan**

○ **the van**

○ **the pan**

○ **the can**

○ **Nan**

○ **Dan**

○ **the van**

○ **the man**

PURPOSES OF THIS PAGE
1. to promote automatic word recognition within phrases
2. to contrast words that differ only in their initial consonants
3. to promote phrase comprehension through picture associations

SECTION 2 LETTER-SOUND CONTENT
Review: CVC spelling pattern -an (fan)
Previously introduced consonant letters
New: Initial consonant letters n, p, v

○ Dan ran to the man.

○ Nan ran to the man.

○ Nan can fan.

○ Dan can fan.

○ Nan ran to the van.

○ Dan ran to the pan.

○ Nan can fan Dan.

○ Dan can fan the man.

PURPOSES OF THIS PAGE
1. to promote automatic word recognition within sentences
2. to promote sentence comprehension through picture associations

SECTION 2 LETTER-SOUND CONTENT
Review: CVC spelling pattern -an (/an/)
Previously introduced consonant letters
New: Initial consonant letters n, p, v

○ The man can fan Dan.

○ Nan can fan Dan.

○ Nan can fan Dan.

○ Nan ran to the man.

○ The man can fan Nan.

○ Nan can fan the man.

○ Dan ran to Nan.

○ Dan ran to the man.

PURPOSES OF THIS PAGE
1. to promote automatic word recognition within sentences
2. to promote sentence comprehension through picture associations

SECTION 2 LETTER-SOUND CONTENT
Review: CVC spelling pattern -an (fan)
Previously introduced consonant letters
New: Initial consonant letters n, p, v

1

2

3

4

PURPOSES OF THIS PAGE
1. to promote automatic word recognition within sentences
2. to promote sentence comprehension through picture associations
3. to give practice in picture interpretation

SECTION 2 LETTER-SOUND CONTENT
Review: CVC spelling pattern -an (fan)
Previously introduced consonant letters
New: Initial consonant letters n, p, v

☐ **Dan can fan the man.**

☐ **The man ran the van.**

☐ **Nan ran to the pan.**

☐ **Dan ran to the van.**

sad

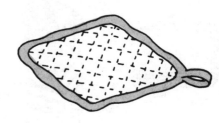

bad

van

pad

Dad

PURPOSES OF THIS PAGE
1. to promote automatic word recognition
2. to promote word comprehension through picture associations

SECTION 3 LETTER-SOUND CONTENT
Review: Previously introduced consonant letters
New: CVC spelling pattern -ad (pad)
Initial consonant letters b, s
Final consonant letter d

pad

sad

Dad

bad

bad

pad

pad

mad

PURPOSES OF THIS PAGE
1. to promote automatic word recognition
2. to contrast words that differ only in their initial or final consonants
3. to promote word comprehension through picture associations

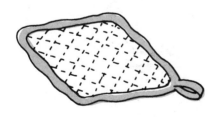

pad

mad

pad

pan

SECTION 3 LETTER-SOUND CONTENT
Review: Previously introduced consonant letters
New: CVC spelling pattern -ad (pad)
Initial consonant letters b, s
Final consonant letter d

○ a sad pad

○ a bad van

○ a tan pad

○ a bad can

○ a tan pad

○ sad Nan

○ mad Dan

○ a sad pan

○ a tan van

○ a bad fan

○ sad Nan

○ sad Dan

PURPOSES OF THIS PAGE
1. to promote automatic word recognition within phrases
2. to contrast words that differ in their initial or final consonants
3. to promote phrase comprehension through picture associations

SECTION 3 LETTER-SOUND CONTENT
Review: Previously introduced consonant letters
New: CVC spelling pattern -ad (pad)
  Initial consonant letters b, s
  Final consonant letter d

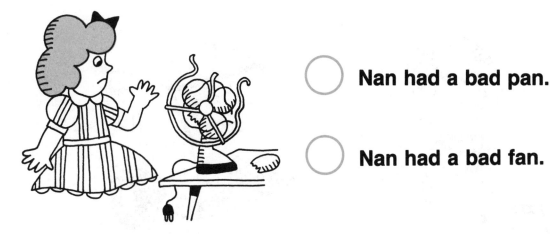

○ Nan had a bad pan.

○ Nan had a bad fan.

○ Nan had a pan.

○ Dad had a pad.

○ Sad Nan ran to Dad.

○ Bad Dan ran to Dad.

○ Sad Dan had a van.

○ Bad Dan had a fan.

1

2

3

4

☐ The man had a van.

☐ Nan had a pad.

☐ Dad had a fan.

☐ Dan had a pan.

PURPOSES OF THIS PAGE
1. to promote automatic word recognition within sentences
2. to promote sentence comprehension through picture associations
3. to give practice in picture interpretation

SECTION 3 LETTER-SOUND CONTENT
Review: Previously introduced consonant letters
New: CVC spelling pattern -ad (pad)
Initial consonant letters b, s
Final consonant letter d

Nan had a
pad.

(pan.)

3

Nan ran to
Dad.

Dan.

Sad Dan had a bad
fan.

van.

Dad had a
pan.

fan.

rag

4 bag

pad

tag

Wag

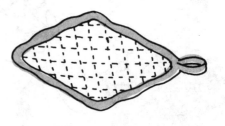

PURPOSES OF THIS PAGE
1. to promote automatic word recognition
2. to promote word comprehension through picture associations

SECTION 4 LETTER-SOUND CONTENT
Review: Previously introduced consonant letters
New: CVC spelling pattern -ag (bag)
     Initial consonant letter w
     Final consonant letter g

Wag

rag

tag

bag

bag

rag

tag

rag

rag

ran

wag

rag

SECTION 4 LETTER-SOUND CONTENT
Review: Previously introduced consonant letters
New: CVC spelling pattern -ag (bag)
Initial consonant letter w
Final consonant letter g

PURPOSES OF THIS PAGE
1. to promote automatic word recognition
2. to contrast words that differ only in their initial or final consonants
3. to promote word comprehension through picture associations

4

○ Nan had a bag.

○ Nan had a rag.

○ Wag can tag.

○ Wag can rag.

○ Nan and Dan ran.

○ Nan had a rag.

○ Wag ran to tag Dan.

○ Wag had a ragbag.

PURPOSES OF THIS PAGE
1. to promote automatic word recognition within sentences
2. to promote sentence comprehension through picture associations

SECTION 4 LETTER-SOUND CONTENT
Review: Previously introduced consonant letters
New: CVC spelling pattern -ag (bag)
Initial consonant letter w
Final consonant letter g

20

1

2

4

3

☐ **Nan had a bag.**

☐ **Dan can tag Wag.**

☐ **Wag had a rag and a bag.**

☐ **Dad ran to tag Dan.**

Wag ran to a ⟨ bag.
rag.

Nan ran to tag ⟨ Dad.
Dan.

Nan ran to a ⟨ rag.
bag.

Dan ran to a sad ⟨ Wag.
rag.

PURPOSES OF THIS PAGE
1. to promote automatic word recognition within sentences
2. to contrast words that differ in their initial or final consonants
3. to promote sentence comprehension through picture associations

SECTION 4 LETTER-SOUND CONTENT
Review: Previously introduced consonant letters
New: CVC spelling pattern -ag (bag)
Initial consonant letter w
Final consonant letter g

4

Can it?

○ Can a rag tag?

○ Can a bag wag?

○ Can a pan tag?

○ Can a pad wag?

○ Can a tag wag?

○ Can a man fan?

○ Can Dan tag Nan?

○ Can Wag wag?

PURPOSES OF THIS PAGE
1. to promote automatic word recognition within sentences that are questions
2. to promote sentence comprehension and interpretation
3. to give practice in detecting absurdities
4. to encourage creative and imaginative responses for discussion

SECTION 4 LETTER-SOUND CONTENT
Review: Previously introduced consonant letters
New: CVC spelling pattern -ag (bag)
   Initial consonant letter w
   Final consonant letter g

4

23

bat

mat

5

rat

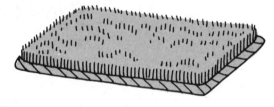

hat

Pat

PURPOSES OF THIS PAGE
1. to promote automatic word recognition
2. to promote word comprehension through picture associations

SECTION 5 LETTER-SOUND CONTENT
Review: Previously introduced consonant letters
New: CVC spelling pattern -at (bat)
Final consonant letter t

cat

rat

bat

Pat

ran

rat

fan

fat

hat

bat

rag

rat

PURPOSES OF THIS PAGE
1. to promote automatic word recognition
2. to contrast words that differ only in their initial or final consonants
3. to promote word comprehension through picture associations

SECTION 5 LETTER-SOUND CONTENT
Review: Previously introduced consonant letters
New: CVC spelling pattern -at (bat)
    Final consonant letter t

a cat and a bag

5

a rat and a hat

Wag and a mat

a cat and a bat

a rag and a rat

PURPOSES OF THIS PAGE
1. to promote automatic word recognition within phrases
2. to promote phrase comprehension through picture associations

SECTION 5 LETTER-SOUND CONTENT
Review: Previously introduced consonant letters
New: CVC spelling pattern -at (bat)
Final consonant letter *t*

○ A cat ran to Dad.

○ A rat ran to Nan.

○ A fat cat ran.

○ A fat cat sat.

○ Pat had a hat.

○ Pat had a bat.

○ A cat can pat the hat.

○ The cat ran to pat the rat.

PURPOSES OF THIS PAGE
1. to promote automatic word recognition within sentences
2. to promote sentence comprehension through picture associations

SECTION 5 LETTER-SOUND CONTENT
Review: Previously introduced consonant letters
New: CVC spelling pattern -at (bat)
Final consonant letter t

1

2

3

4

PURPOSES OF THIS PAGE
1. to promote automatic word recognition within sentences
2. to promote sentence comprehension through picture associations
3. to give practice in picture interpretation

☐ **Dad had a hat.**

☐ **Wag ran to the cat.**

☐ **Dan and Dad can bat.**

☐ **Pat had a cat and a mat.**

SECTION 5 LETTER-SOUND CONTENT
Review: Previously introduced consonant letters
New: CVC spelling pattern -at (bat)
Final consonant letter t

Pat ran to pat the

cat.

rat.

The cat ran at a fat

hat.

rat.

Dan can pat a fat

cat.

bat.

The cat sat at a

mat.

hat.

PURPOSES OF THIS PAGE
1. to promote automatic word recognition within sentences
2. to contrast words that differ only in their initial consonants
3. to promote sentence comprehension through picture associations

SECTION 5 LETTER-SOUND CONTENT
Review: Previously introduced consonant letters
New: CVC spelling pattern -at (bat)
Final consonant letter t

Can it?

○ Can a bat pat a hat?

○ Can a mat bat a hat?

○ Can a pad pat a pan?

○ Can a cat bat a hat?

○ Can a rat pat a cat?

○ Can a cat tag a rat?

○ Can Pat tag Wag?

○ Can Dad and Dan bat?

PURPOSES OF THIS PAGE
1. to promote automatic word recognition within sentences that are questions
2. to promote sentence comprehension and interpretation
3. to give practice in detecting absurdities
4. to encourage creative and imaginative responses for discussion

SECTION 5 LETTER-SOUND CONTENT
Review: Previously introduced consonant letters
New: CVC spelling pattern -at (bat)
      Final consonant letter t

5

SECTION 6 LETTER-SOUND CONTENT
Review: Previously introduced consonant letters
New: CVC spelling pattern -ap (cap)
Initial consonant letter l
Final consonant letter p

PURPOSES OF THIS PAGE
1. to promote automatic word recognition within phrases
2. to promote phrase comprehension through picture associations

☐ **a cap**

☐ **a map**

☐ **to tap**

☐ **to nap**

☐ **a lap**

1

2

3

4

5

6

31

 cap
cat

 tap
lap

 tap
tag

 rap
rag

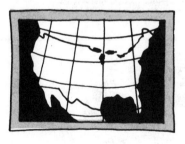 map
mat

 nap
nag

PURPOSES OF THIS PAGE
1. to promote automatic word recognition
2. to contrast words that differ only in their initial or final consonants
3. to promote word comprehension through picture associations

6

SECTION 6 LETTER-SOUND CONTENT
Review: Previously introduced consonant letters
New: CVC spelling pattern -ap (cap)
Initial consonant letter l
Final consonant letter p

PURPOSES OF THIS PAGE
1. to promote automatic word recognition within phrases
2. to promote phrase comprehension through picture associations

□ **a cap and a fan**

□ **a rag and a pad**

□ **a cap and a map**

□ **a bag and a mat**

□ **to tap and to rap**

SECTION 6 LETTER-SOUND CONTENT
Review: Previously introduced consonant letters
New: CVC spelling pattern -ap (cap)
Initial consonant letter /
Final consonant letter p

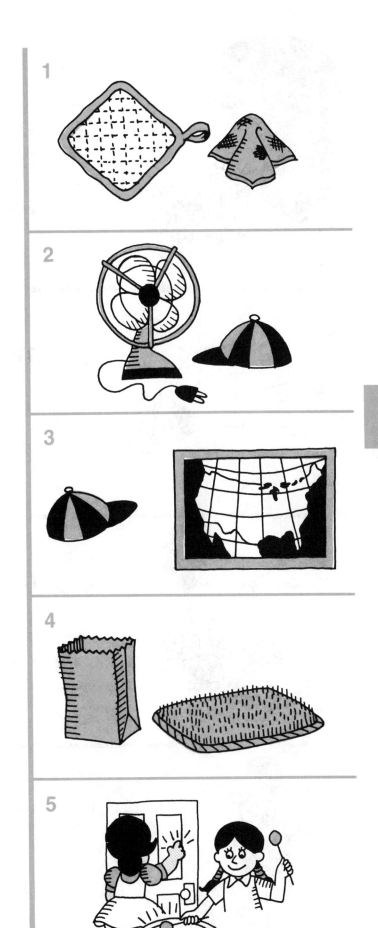

6

33

○ Wag had a nap.

○ Pat had a map.

○ The cat had the cap.

○ The rat had the map.

6

○ Dan had a map.

○ Dad had a hat.

○ Wag can tap Dad.

○ Dan can tap the bat.

PURPOSES OF THIS PAGE
1. To promote automatic word recognition within sentences
2. To promote sentence comprehension through picture associations

SECTION 6 LETTER-SOUND CONTENT
Review: Previously introduced consonant letters
New: CVC spelling pattern *-ap* (*cap*)
Initial consonant letter *l*
Final consonant letter *p*

6

☐ The fat cat had a hat.

☐ Dan can tap the bat.

☐ The fat cat had a bag.

☐ The fat cat had a nap.

Nan had a cap and a

map.

nap.

Dad sat and had a

map.

nap.

Wag can tap the

pad.

pan.

Pat had to rap and

tap.

nap.

Can it?

○ Can a map tap a mat?

○ Can a bat tap a can?

○ Can a cap tap a cat?

○ Can a lap nap and tap?

○ Can Nan tap and rap?

○ Can a man tap a cap?

○ Can a cat map?

○ Can a man nap?

PURPOSES OF THIS PAGE
1. to promote automatic word recognition within sentences that are questions
2. to promote sentence comprehension and interpretation
3. to give practice in detecting absurdities
4. to encourage creative and imaginative responses for discussion

SECTION 6 LETTER-SOUND CONTENT
Review: Previously introduced consonant letters
New: CVC spelling pattern -ap (cap)
    Initial consonant letter l
    Final consonant letter p

6

☐ **Sam**

☐ **jam**

7

☐ **hat**

☐ **ham**

☐ **Pam**

1

2

3

4

5

PURPOSES OF THIS PAGE
1. to promote automatic word recognition
2. to promote word comprehension through picture associations

SECTION 7 LETTER-SOUND CONTENT
Review: Previously introduced consonant letters
New: CVC spelling pattern -am (jam)
Initial consonant letter j
Final consonant letter m

 cat
cap

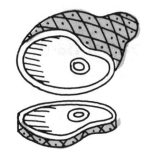 ham
hat

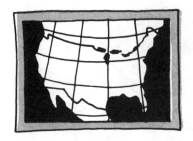 map
mat

 pan
Pam

7

 sat
Sam

 jam
ham

PURPOSES OF THIS PAGE
1. to promote automatic word recognition
2. to contrast words that differ only in their initial or final consonants
3. to promote word comprehension through picture associations

SECTION 7 LETTER-SOUND CONTENT
Review: Previously introduced consonant letters
New: CVC spelling pattern -am (jam)
    Initial consonant letter j
    Final consonant letter m

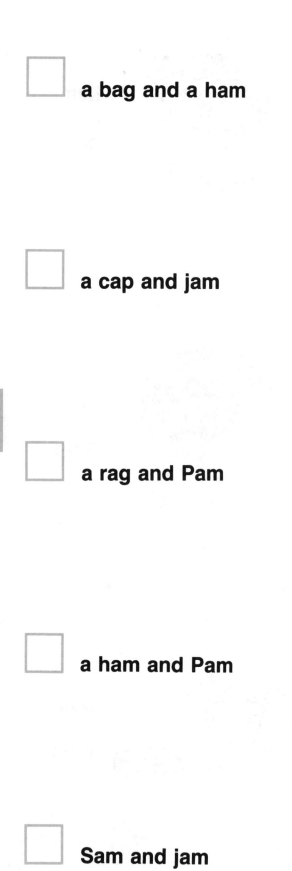

□ a bag and a ham

□ a cap and jam

7

□ a rag and Pam

□ a ham and Pam

□ Sam and jam

1

2

3

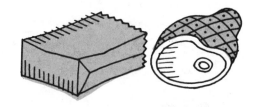

4

5

PURPOSES OF THIS PAGE
1. to promote automatic word recognition within phrases
2. to promote phrase comprehension through picture associations

SECTION 7 LETTER-SOUND CONTENT
Review: Previously introduced consonant letters
New: CVC spelling pattern -am (jam)
Initial consonant letter j
Final consonant letter m

○ Dad had a can of jam.

○ Pam had a pan of jam.

○ Wag had a pan of ham.

○ Sam had a tan hat.

○ I am Sam.

○ I am Pam.

○ Sam had a nap.

○ Pam had a map.

7

1

2

3

4

7

☐ Wag ran to tag a rat.

☐ Pam and Wag had a nap.

☐ Wag can tap the ham.

☐ Sam sat and had jam and ham.

PURPOSES OF THIS PAGE
1. to promote automatic word recognition within sentences
2. to promote sentence comprehension through picture associations
3. to give practice in picture interpretation

SECTION 7 LETTER-SOUND CONTENT
Review: Previously introduced consonant letters
New: CVC spelling pattern -am (jam)
Initial consonant letter j
Final consonant letter m

hat.

I had a can of

ham.

Sam

Wag ran to Dan and

Pam

jam.

Wag can tap the can of

rags.

Dan.

Sam ran to

Pam.

PURPOSES OF THIS PAGE
1. to promote automatic word recognition within sentences
2. to contrast words of similar spelling and configuration
3. to promote sentence comprehension through picture association

SECTION 7 LETTER-SOUND CONTENT
Review: Previously introduced consonant letters
New: CVC spelling pattern -am (jam)
Initial consonant letter j
Final consonant letter m

43

I am a man.

I ran a van.

I had a hat.

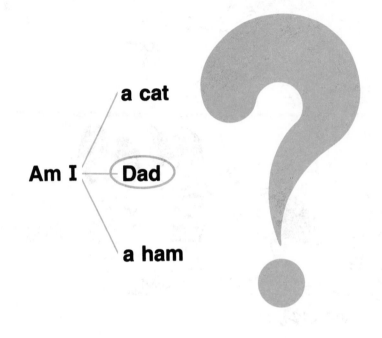

a cat

Am I — ⟨Dad⟩

a ham

I am tan.

I can nap.

I can tag a rat.

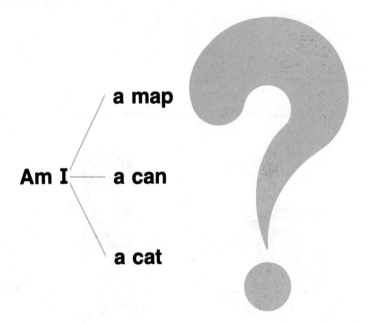

a map

Am I — a can

a cat

PURPOSES OF THIS PAGE
1. to promote automatic word recognition within sentences
2. to contrast phrases containing words of similar spelling and configuration
3. to promote sentence and paragraph comprehension
4. to give practice in reasoning logically and drawing conclusions

SECTION 7 LETTER-SOUND CONTENT
Review: Previously introduced consonant letters
New: CVC spelling pattern -am (jam)
Initial consonant letter j
Final consonant letter m

☐ **Sal**

☐ **Al**

☐ **cab**

☐ **jab**

☐ **jam**

1

2

3

8

4

5

45

○ **Pam's jam**

○ **Dad's jab**

○ **Val's cap**

○ **Val's cab**

○ **Wag's pal**

○ **Wag's pan**

○ **Wag's hat**

○ **Wag's ham**

○ **Al's cab**

○ **Al's cap**

○ **Pam's lap**

○ **Pam's pal**

PURPOSES OF THIS PAGE
1. to promote automatic word recognition within phrases
2. to contrast words of similar spelling and configuration
3. to promote phrase comprehension through picture associations

SECTION 8 LETTER-SOUND CONTENT
Review: Previously introduced consonant letters
New: CVC spelling patterns -ab (cab) and -al (pal)
Final consonant letters b and l

46

PURPOSES OF THIS PAGE
1. to promote automatic word recognition within phrases
2. to promote phrase comprehension through picture associations

SECTION 8 LETTER-SOUND CONTENT
Review: Previously introduced consonant letters
New: CVC spelling patterns -ab (cab) and -al (pal)
Final consonant letters b and l

☐ **Nan and Pam**

☐ **Dan and Sam**

☐ **Dad and Sal**

☐ **Dad and Sam**

☐ **Wag and a pal**

8

○ Pam has a tan bat.

○ Pam has a mad hat.

○ Al has a map.

○ Val ran a cab.

○ Bad Wag ran to jab the bag.

○ Sad Sal ran to pat the bag.

○ Wag ran to Al's pal.

○ Wag ran to Al's lap.

8

PURPOSES OF THIS PAGE
1. to promote automatic word recognition within sentences
2. to promote sentence comprehension through picture associations

SECTION 8 LETTER-SOUND CONTENT
Review: Previously introduced consonant letters
New: CVC spelling patterns -ab (cab) and -al (pal)
Final consonant letters b and l

1

2

3

4

PURPOSES OF THIS PAGE
1. to promote automatic word recognition within sentences
2. to promote sentence comprehension through picture associations
3. to give practice in picture interpretation

SECTION 8 LETTER-SOUND CONTENT
Review: Previously introduced consonant letters
New: CVC spelling patterns -ab (cab) and -al (pal)
Final consonant letters b and l

☐ Al has a bag.

☐ Wag has a pal.

☐ I had a cab and a map.

☐ Hal has a van and a cap.

49

Pam has a pan and a

pad.

pal.

Val has a cab and a

pan.

pal.

cat.

Hal has a van and a

cap.

Al has a rag and a

cap.

cab.

PURPOSES OF THIS PAGE
1. to promote automatic word recognition within sentences
2. to contrast words that differ only in their final consonants
3. to promote sentence comprehension through picture associations

SECTION 8 LETTER-SOUND CONTENT
Review: Previously introduced consonant letters
New: CVC spelling patterns -ab (cab) and -al (pal)
Final consonant letters b and l

I am Sal's pal.

I can run and tag.

I had a mad hat.

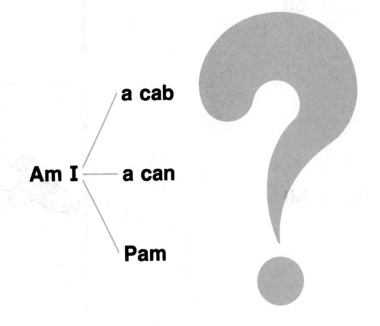

Am I — a cab
Am I — a can
Am I — Pam

8

I am Sam's pal.

I can tag and bat.

I had a cap.

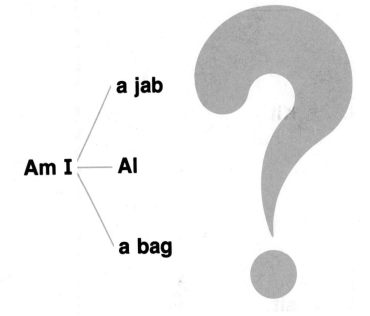

Am I — a jab
Am I — Al
Am I — a bag

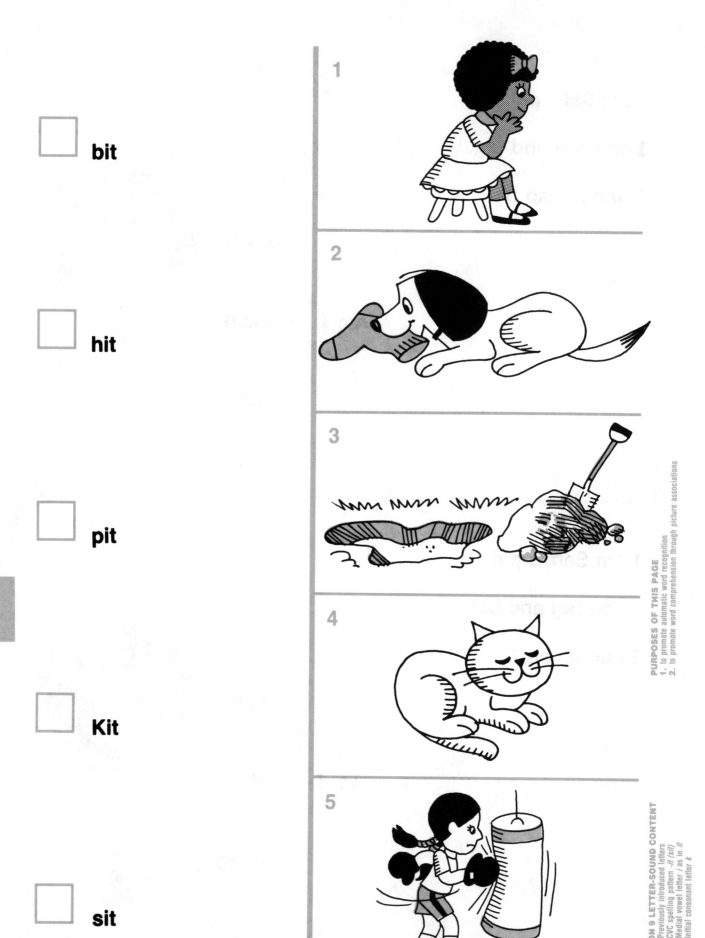

☐ bit

☐ hit

☐ pit

☐ Kit

☐ sit

9

1

2

3

4

5

PURPOSES OF THIS PAGE
1. to promote automatic word recognition
2. to promote word comprehension through picture associations

SECTION 9 LETTER-SOUND CONTENT
Review: Previously introduced letters
New: CVC spelling pattern -*it* (*sit*)
Medial vowel letter *i* as in *it*
Initial consonant letter *k*

○ **A bat hits.**

○ **A hat fits.**

○ **A rat sits.**

○ **A bat hits.**

○ **Kit the cat naps.**

○ **Kit the cat bit.**

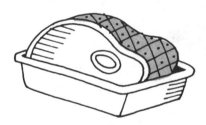

○ **A bag sits.**

○ **A ham fits.**

9

○ **A pal bit.**

○ **A pal sits.**

○ **Kit the cat bit.**

○ **Kit the cat hits.**

○ Pam ran and lit it.

○ Sam had to fit it.

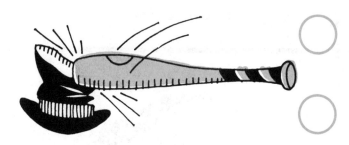

○ Dan's bat hit the hat.

○ Dan's cat bit the rat.

○ Sal can sit and pat Kit.

○ Sal can sit at the pit.

○ Kit the cat can sit.

○ Wag bit the fat ham.

PURPOSES OF THIS PAGE
1. to promote automatic word recognition within sentences
2. to promote sentence comprehension through picture associations

SECTION 9 LETTER-SOUND CONTENT
Review: Previously introduced letters
New: CVC spelling pattern -it (sit)
Medial vowel letter i as in it
Initial consonant letter k

1

2

3

4

9

☐ **The hat and the cap fit Al.**

☐ **Sal and Kit can sit.**

☐ **Kit ran to a pit.**

☐ **The rat sits and hits it.**

Kit and Wag can

sit.

hit.

Wag had a

hit.

hat.

9

Wag bit a

bat.

bit.

Pam can sit at a

pat.

pit.

Can it?

○ Can a cat sit and nap?

○ Can a pit sit and nap?

○ Can a hat fit a man?

○ Can a ham fit Sam?

○ Can a bat tap and hit?

○ Can a rat sit and hit?

○ Can a map fit a kit?

○ Can a cat fit a pit?

PURPOSES OF THIS PAGE
1. to promote automatic word recognition within sentences that are questions
2. to promote sentence comprehension and interpretation
3. to give practice in detecting absurdities
4. to encourage creative and imaginative responses for discussion

SECTION 9 LETTER-SOUND CONTENT
Review: Previously introduced letters
New: CVC spelling pattern -it (sit)
Medial vowel letter i as in it
Initial consonant letter k

9

I can sit.

I can nap.

I ran and bit a rat.

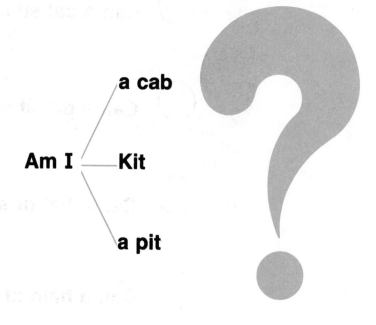

Am I
- a cab
- Kit
- a pit

I am tan.

I can fit Sam.

I can fit Al.

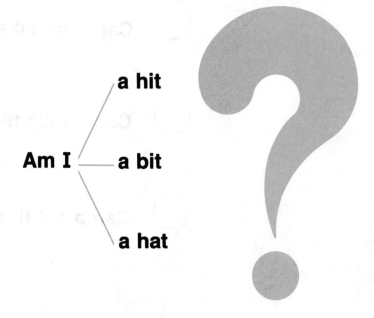

Am I
- a hit
- a bit
- a hat

9

PURPOSES OF THIS PAGE
1. to promote automatic word recognition within sentences
2. to contrast phrases containing words of similar spelling and configuration
3. to promote sentence and paragraph comprehension
4. to give practice in reasoning logically and drawing conclusions

SECTION 9 LETTER-SOUND CONTENT
Review: Previously introduced letters
New: CVC spelling pattern -it (sit)
Medial vowel letter i as in it
Initial consonant letter k

□ a pin

□ to win

□ a tin can

□ a tin van

□ a tin pan

PURPOSES OF THIS PAGE
1. to promote automatic word recognition within phrases
2. to promote phrase comprehension through picture associations

SECTION 10 LETTER-SOUND CONTENT
Review: Previously introduced letters
New: CVC spelling pattern -in (pin)

1

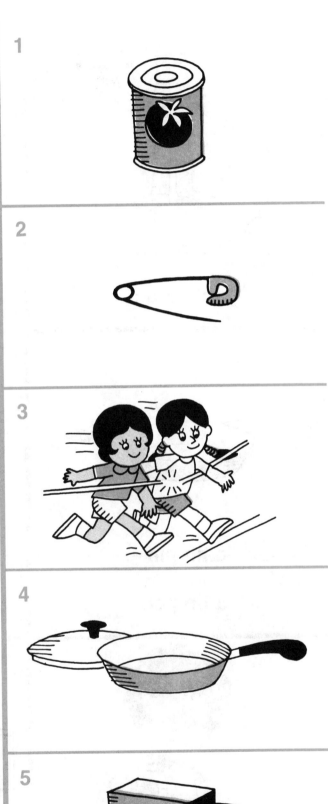

2

3

4

10

5

○ **a tan van**

○ **a tin man**

○ **a tan pan**

○ **a tin can**

○ **a tin pin**

○ **a tin pan**

○ **Al's tin van**

○ **Sal's tin pan**

○ **Sam wins it.**

○ **Sal pins it.**

○ **Kit is in it.**

○ **Kit ran to it.**

10

PURPOSES OF THIS PAGE
1. to promote automatic word recognition within phrases and sentences
2. to contrast words of similar spelling and configuration
3. to promote phrase and sentence comprehension through picture associations

SECTION 10 LETTER-SOUND CONTENT
Review: Previously introduced letters
New: CVC spelling pattern -in (pin)

○ Kit has a tin can of jam.

○ Kit ran to win at tag.

○ Dad has a pin in his cap.

○ Dad has a cat in his lap.

○ The pin fits in Nan's hat.

○ The map fits into Al's cab.

○ Kit sat in a hat.

○ Pat ran into a pin.

PURPOSES OF THIS PAGE
1. to promote automatic word recognition within sentences
2. to promote sentence comprehension through picture associations

SECTION 10 LETTER-SOUND CONTENT
Review: Previously introduced letters
New: CVC spelling pattern -in (pin)

☐ **Kit is in a pit.**

☐ **Kit is in a tin pan.**

☐ **Kit is in a hat.**

☐ **Kit is in a lap.**

PURPOSES OF THIS PAGE
1. to promote automatic word recognition within sentences
2. to promote sentence comprehension through picture associations
3. to give practice in picture interpretation

SECTION 10 LETTER-SOUND CONTENT
Review: Previously introduced letters
New: CVC spelling pattern -in (pin)

Kit the cat is in Dad's

cap.

lap.

Kit the cat has a tin

pin.

pan.

Kit the cat can fit in a

cab.

can.

10

Kit can fit in a tin

pin.

pan.

SECTION 10 LETTER-SOUND CONTENT
Review: Previously introduced letters
New: CVC spelling pattern -in (pin)

63

Can it?

○ Can a pin fit in a hat?

○ Can a pin fit in a tin can?

○ Can a pin sit in a pit?

○ Can a tin pan fit a man?

○ Can a tin van fit a man?

○ Can Kit the cat fit in a pit?

○ Can Kit the cat fit in Dad's lap?

○ Can Kit the cat fit in a cab?

PURPOSES OF THIS PAGE
1. to promote automatic word recognition within sentences that are questions
2. to promote sentence comprehension and interpretation
3. to give practice in detecting absurdities
4. to encourage creative and imaginative responses for discussion

SECTION 10 LETTER-SOUND CONTENT
Review: Previously introduced letters
New: CVC spelling pattern -in (pin)

It can bat.

It can tag.

It can win.

Is it
- a pan
- a pin
- Al

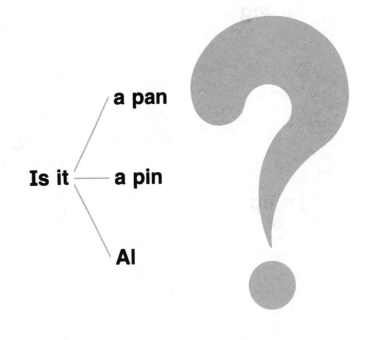

PURPOSES OF THIS PAGE
1. to promote automatic word recognition within sentences
2. to contrast phrases containing words of similar spelling and configuration
3. to promote sentence and paragraph comprehension
4. to give practice in reasoning logically and drawing conclusions

It can sit in a hat.

It can tag a rat.

It can nap in Nan's lap.

10

Is it
- a pit
- a cat
- a cab

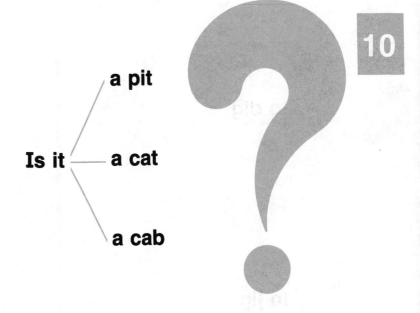

SECTION 10 LETTER-SOUND CONTENT
Review: Previously introduced letters
New: CVC spelling pattern -in (pin)

□ a wig

□ a fig

□ a pig

11 □ to dig

□ to jig

1

2

3

4

5

○ **a big wig**

○ **a big wag**

○ **a big pit**

○ **a big pig**

○ **a sad pig**

○ **a fat fig**

○ **a big wag**

○ **a big wig**

PURPOSES OF THIS PAGE
1. to promote automatic word recognition within phrases and sentences
2. to contrast words of similar spelling and configuration
3. to promote phrase and sentence comprehension through picture associations

○ **Kit can dig.**

○ **Pat can jig.**

○ **The pig jigs.**

○ **The pig digs.**

11

SECTION 11 LETTER-SOUND CONTENT
Review: Previously introduced letters
New: CVC spelling pattern -ig (pig)

○ The tin man is big.

○ The big man can dig.

○ Dan can bat and win.

○ Dan has a bat and a fig.

○ Wag and Kit can dig in a pit.

○ Sam and Sal can sit in a pit.

11

○ Pam fits a pin in a wig.

○ Pam has a wig and a hat.

PURPOSES OF THIS PAGE
1. to promote automatic word recognition within sentences
2. to promote sentence comprehension through picture associations

SECTION 11 LETTER-SOUND CONTENT
Review: Previously introduced letters
New: CVC spelling pattern -ig (pig)

1

2

3

4

PURPOSES OF THIS PAGE
1. to promote automatic word recognition within sentences
2. to promote sentence comprehension through picture associations
3. to give practice in picture interpretation

☐ **A pig can jig.**

☐ **A pig can win.**

☐ **A pig can dig.**

☐ **A pig can sit.**

SECTION 11 LETTER-SOUND CONTENT
Review: Previously introduced letters
New: CVC spelling pattern -ig (pig)

11

wig.

Wag can

wag.

hat.

Kit wins a

hit.

jig.

The pig can

dig.

pit.

Kit can dig a big

bit.

PURPOSES OF THIS PAGE
1. to promote automatic word recognition within sentences
2. to contrast words of similar spelling and configuration
3. to promote sentence comprehension through picture associations

SECTION 11 LETTER-SOUND CONTENT
Review: Previously introduced letters
New: CVC spelling pattern -ig (pig)

It is a pal.

It can dig.

It can sit in Sam's lap.

Is it ——— a wig

Is it ——— Wag

Is it ——— a fig

PURPOSES OF THIS PAGE
1. to promote automatic word recognition within sentences
2. to contrast phrases containing words of similar spelling and configuration
3. to promote sentence and paragraph comprehension
4. to give practice in reasoning logically and drawing conclusions

It is big.

A pig can dig it.

Kit can dig in it.

Is it ——— a pig

Is it ——— a pin

Is it ——— a pit

11

SECTION 11 LETTER-SOUND CONTENT
Review: Previously introduced letters
New: CVC spelling pattern -ig (pig)

Dad is	⊗	a big man.
	◯	a tin man.
Wag is as big as	◯	the mat.
	◯	the man.
Nan has	◯	a big hat.
	◯	a tin wig.
Nan can	◯	jig in a big hat.
	◯	dig in a big pit.

PURPOSES OF THIS PAGE
1. to promote automatic word recognition within sentences
2. to contrast phrases containing words of similar spelling and configuration
3. to promote sentence comprehension through picture associations
4. to give practice in picture interpretation

SECTION 11 LETTER-SOUND CONTENT
Review: Previously introduced letters
New: CVC spelling pattern -ig (pig)

PURPOSES OF THIS PAGE
1. to promote automatic word recognition
2. to promote word comprehension through picture associations

☐ **Sid**

☐ **sit**

☐ **lid**

☐ **hid**

☐ **wig**

SECTION 12 LETTER-SOUND CONTENT
Review: Previously introduced letters
New: CVC spelling pattern *-id (lid)*

12

73

lid

lit

lad

hid

hit

had

Sid

sad

sit

sad

sit

Sid

did

dad

dig

hit

hid

had

12

○ Sid hid his bat in a bag.

○ Sid did a jig in a pit.

○ The tin pin fits into the pan.

○ The tin pan has a big lid.

○ Sid hid the cat in his lap.

○ The fat cat hid in the bag.

○ The pig did a jig in a lid.

○ The pig began to dig in a pit.

12

1

2

3

4

PURPOSES OF THIS PAGE
1. to promote automatic word recognition within sentences
2. to promote sentence comprehension through picture associations
3. to give practice in picture interpretation

☐ **Sid hid the lid.**

☐ **Sid did a jig.**

☐ **Sid and Dan hid.**

☐ **The pig hid in a pit.**

12

SECTION 12 LETTER-SOUND CONTENT
Review: Previously introduced letters
New: CVC spelling pattern -*id* (*lid*)

PURPOSES OF THIS PAGE
1. to promote automatic word recognition within sentences
2. to contrast words of similar spelling and configuration
3. to promote sentence comprehension through picture associations

Sal hid the lid in a

big.

bag.

Pam hid the pin in a

wag.

wig.

Sid hid his tin pig in a

pat.

pit.

Dad hid a map in his

lid.

kit.

12

SECTION 12 LETTER-SOUND CONTENT
Review: Previously introduced letters
New: CVC spelling pattern -id (lid)

77

Can it?

◯ **Can a wig fit a pig?**

◯ **Can a wig fit Pam?**

◯ **Can a lid fit a tin pan?**

◯ **Can a big pig dig in a pit?**

◯ **Can a big pig sit in a lid?**

◯ **Can Sid jig in a wig?**

◯ **Can Wag wag his wig?**

◯ **Can Sid hit the lid Dan hid?**

12

78

PURPOSES OF THIS PAGE
1. to promote automatic word recognition within sentences that are questions
2. to promote sentence comprehension and interpretation
3. to give practice in detecting absurdities
4. to encourage creative and imaginative responses for discussion

SECTION 12 LETTER-SOUND CONTENT
Review: Previously introduced letters
New: CVC spelling pattern -id (lid)

Sid's pals hid Sid's bat in a
- ◯ tin can.
- ◯ tan bag.

Sid is mad at
- ◯ his pals.
- ◉ his lid.

Wag is as mad as
- ◯ Sid
- ◯ the lid.

As his pals ran, Sid had to dig
- ◯ in the tin pan.
- ◯ in the tin can.

12

☐ **Kit**

☐ **Kim**

☐ **rim**

☐ **Jim**

☐ **jam**

PURPOSES OF THIS PAGE
1. to promote automatic word recognition
2. to promote word comprehension through picture associations

SECTION 13 LETTER-SOUND CONTENT
Review: Previously introduced letters
New: CVC spelling pattern -im (him)

ham

him

hid

tin

Tim

tan

Tim

tin

tan

ran

rag

rim

Jim

jam

Kim

hit

Kit

Kim

13

○ **Jim's pal**
○ **Jim's lap**

○ **Kim's pan**
○ **Kim's pal**

○ **Tim's ham**
○ **Tim's him**

○ **Sid's rim**
○ **Sid's lid**

○ **Kim's wag**
○ **Kim's wig**

○ **Kit's pit**
○ **Kit's pin**

PURPOSES OF THIS PAGE
1. to promote automatic word recognition within phrases
2. to contrast words of similar spelling and configuration
3. to promote phrase comprehension through picture associations

SECTION 13 LETTER-SOUND CONTENT
Review: Previously introduced letters
New: CVC spelling pattern -*im (him)*

13

○ A fat pig bit Tim.

○ A fat pig can dig.

○ A pig hid him.

○ The pig did a jig.

○ A pig ran into him.

○ Jim has a fat pig.

○ A lid fits the rim of the pan.

○ Jim hid the rim of the pan.

13

1

2

3

4

PURPOSES OF THIS PAGE
1. to promote automatic word recognition within sentences
2. to promote sentence comprehension through picture associations
3. to give practice in picture interpretation

☐ **Kit sits at his pit.**

☐ **Kim has a big wig.**

☐ **Tim has his big ham.**

☐ **Jim hid his big bat.**

SECTION 13 LETTER-SOUND CONTENT
Review: Previously introduced letters
New: CVC spelling pattern -im (him)

13

PURPOSES OF THIS PAGE
1. to promote automatic word recognition within sentences
2. to contrast phrases containing words of similar spelling and configuration
3. to promote sentence comprehension through picture associations
4. to give practice in picture interpretation

Kit the cat ran to   ◯ **Tim.**

◯ **Kim.**

As Tim naps, Kit can pat   ◯ **him.**

◯ **Kim.**

Wag sits   ◯ **in a tin pan.**

◯ **in a big pit.**

Tim's pal began to   ◯ **dig a big pit.**

◯ **sit in a big pit.**

SECTION 13 LETTER-SOUND CONTENT
Review: Previously introduced letters
New: CVC spelling pattern -im (him)

13

If it fits the rim of a pan,

it is

Wag

Kit

Kim

a lid

If it can dig and bat,

it is

Tim

a fig

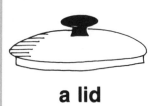

a pin

a lid

If it can sit and nap,

it is

a cab

jam

a cap

Jim

13

86

PURPOSES OF THIS PAGE
1. to promote automatic word recognition within sentences
2. to promote sentence comprehension through picture associations

SECTION 13 LETTER-SOUND CONTENT
Review: Previously introduced letters
New: CVC spelling pattern -im (him)

rip

dip

sip

zip

tip

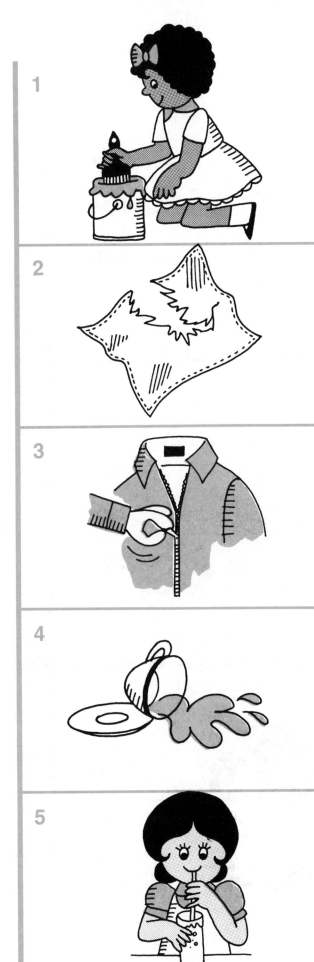

14

87

lids

lips

laps

dips

hips

pits

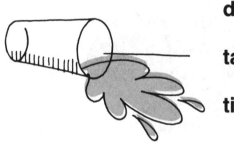

dips

taps

tips

rap

rip

sip

zips

sips

zigs

tips

digs

dips

PURPOSES OF THIS PAGE
1. to promote automatic word recognition
2. to contrast several words of similar spelling and configuration
3. to promote word comprehension through picture associations

SECTION 14 LETTER-SOUND CONTENT
Review: Previously introduced letters
New: CVC spelling pattern -ip (lip)
Initial consonant letter z

14

○ Jim can dip it.

○ Tim can sip it.

○ Jim had to rip it.

○ Sid had to zip it.

○ Tim hid his lips.

○ Jim hid his hips.

○ The pin began to rip it.

○ The pan began to tip.

PURPOSES OF THIS PAGE
1. to promote automatic word recognition within sentences
2. to promote sentence comprehension through picture associations

SECTION 14 LETTER-SOUND CONTENT
Review: Previously introduced letters
New: CVC spelling pattern -ip (tip)
Initial consonant letter z

14

1

2

3

4

□ Kim can tip the hat.

□ Sid began to rip the rag.

□ Kim began to tip the pan.

□ Jim began to zip the bag.

SECTION 14 LETTER-SOUND CONTENT
Review: Previously introduced letters
New: CVC spelling pattern -ip (lip)
Initial consonant letter z

PURPOSES OF THIS PAGE
1. to promote automatic word recognition within sentences
2. to promote sentence comprehension through picture associations
3. to give practice in picture interpretation

14